HIS HOLINESS THE 17ᵀᴴ GYALWANG KARMAPA · OGYEN TRINLEY DORJE

THE FUTURE IS NOW

TIMELY ADVICE FOR CREATING A BETTER WORLD

THE ACADEMY OF EVERYTHING IS POSSIBLE

HAY HOUSE, INC.

HAY HOUSE, INC.
CARLSBAD, CALIFORNIA • NEW YORK CITY • LONDON • SYDNEY
JOHANNESBURG • VANCOUVER • HONG KONG • NEW DELHI

Published and distributed in the United States by: Hay House, Inc.: www.hayhouse.com
Published and distributed in Australia by: Hay House Australia Pty. Ltd.: www.hayhouse.com.au
Published and distributed in the United Kingdom by: Hay House UK, Ltd.: www.hayhouse.co.uk
Published in India by: Hay House Publishers India: www.hayhouse.co.in
Published and distributed in the Republic of South Africa by: Hay House SA (Pty), Ltd.: www.hayhouse.co.za
Distributed in Canada by: Raincoast: www.raincoast.com

Concept: Gordon Campbell at www.theacademyofeverythingispossible.info
Book Design and Image Selection: Paul O'Connor
Translation: Ven. Ringu Tulku Rinpoche
Project Management: Paula Litzky

Library of Congress Cataloging-in-Publication Data

O-rgyan-'phrin-las-rdo-rje, Karma-pa XVII, 1985-The future is now : timely advice for creating a better world / His Holiness the Seventeenth Gyalwang Karmapa, Ogyen Trinley Dorje.
    p. cm.
ISBN 978-1-4019-2300-6 (pbk. : alk. paper) 1. Religious life--Buddhism. 2. Buddhism--Doctrines. 3. Kar-ma-pa (Sect)--Doctrines. I. Title.
 BQ5395.O74 2009
 294.3'44--dc22

                                    2008051456

ISBN: 978-1-4019-2300-6

12 11 10 09 4 3 2 1
1st edition, May 2009

Printed in Korea

HOMAGE

The poison and enemy of this world,
he declared, is the growth of poison in the mind.
He cut off that growth with the sword of wisdom.

The father and mother of this world,
he declared, are the countless sentient beings,
and he nurtured them with love and compassion.

The joy and misery of this world,
he declared, is the result of our own karma,
and he showed us the ways to purify it.

The refuge and guide of this world,
I understand, is the Prince of the Sakya,
and I humbly prostrate myself at his feet.

CONTENTS

MESSAGE FROM HIS HOLINESS THE DALAI LAMA

I would like to express my appreciation and delight that the Seventeenth Karmapa, Ogyen Trinley Dorje, the supreme head of the practice lineage, has composed 108 sayings of advice at the request of some devoted individuals.

From a young age, the Seventeenth Karmapa displayed the signs of a noble and holy being. While residing in Tibet and since his escape, he has engaged in numerous activities to benefit the general public and specific individuals, as well as the teachings of Buddha and specific Buddhist schools. The Seventeenth Karmapa's sincere and beneficial activities, performed with the highest intentions, continue to expand.

I pray to the Three Jewels that this book of sayings, composed for people

MY MESSAGE

I am not someone entirely free of malice. Nonetheless, since I have studied
a bit about Buddhism, now and then the wish to benefit all beings arises
in me. I am writing this book inspired by that attitude, untainted by selfish
motives. For the most part, at least 90 percent of the time, I have tried to
base my explanations on facts. While I am neither a scholar nor a great
thinker, what I have said comes from my heart and I have said it as directly
as possible. Perhaps both young and old may find something useful here.
Even if you find nothing useful in this book, please do not be angry.
You can always throw it away!

The Seventeenth Karmapa,
Ogyen Trinley Dorje

THE POINT OF ADVICE

Ideally, advice is instruction tailored to the circumstances, both immediate and long-term. The person giving advice should have the motivation to help others and the wisdom to distinguish right from wrong. The person receiving it should have the intelligence to understand it and the willingness to follow directions. It should be presented in just the right way, so that it is relevant to the situation at hand and easy to understand. Whatever it takes—either gently or harshly! Once the recipient sees both the benefits and the drawbacks of a course of action, the advice has accomplished its purpose.

DIALOGUE

When you pose a question, you are simply
asking for what comes to mind spontaneously
as a response. Likewise, in reply I only state
whatever comes to mind at that very moment.
It is a spontaneous exchange. Apart from this,
there is no true dialogue.

GUIDANCE

Each person must find his or her own path.
Nonetheless, seek guidance from wise and
compassionate people and listen to them
earnestly. This will help you find the best
way to proceed—now and in the future.

FUTURE PROSPECTS

The future of our society depends on today's youth. If young people have enthusiasm for education, ethics, and peace, we have a solid foundation for progress. If not, the basis for a good future is missing.

HUMAN LIFE

Whether or not we believe in reincarnation, we can each live a purposeful life if we spend our time doing something beneficial for ourselves and others. At the very least, we need to find a way to lead our lives joyfully. But if we do the opposite—what a shame! If we only create misery, we have wasted our lives. What's more, all the trouble that others have gone through to feed and clothe us becomes pointless.

INTELLIGENCE

Human beings are the most intelligent and resourceful species on earth. If we use our intelligence to cause more suffering, rather than to bring some real benefit to others and ourselves, we are no better than beasts.

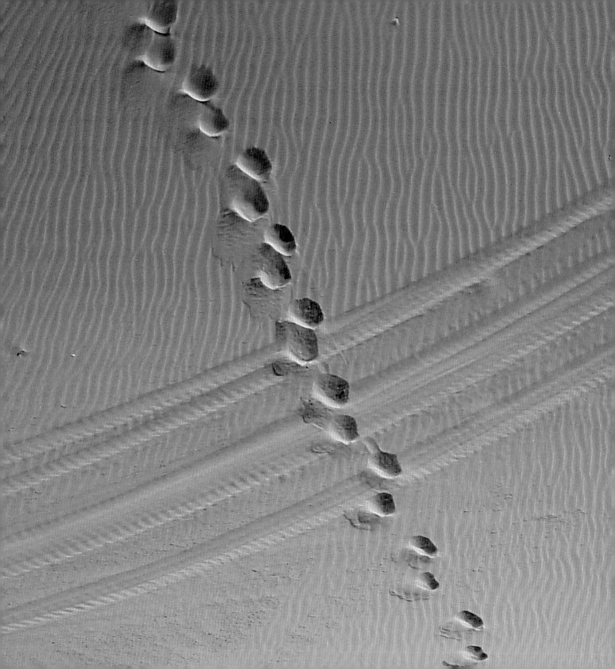

LEGACY

If we do not leave a good legacy for the
next generation, we have walked this earth
in vain. What a wasted opportunity!

TRADITION

All traditions, whether religious or secular,
have developed to benefit human society.
In the event that a tradition or system
becomes harmful, there's no need to
insist on following it.

REACTIONS

Our misery or happiness depends on how we
react to external events and internal thoughts.
We judge and label everything based on our
reactions. Sometimes our reactions are so strong
that they destroy us. But the real problem is in not
understanding that reactions themselves come
and go based on ever-changing circumstances.

BE YOUR OWN GUIDE

Whether or not you go in a positive direction depends entirely on you. You have to be your own teacher and try to figure out what it takes to accomplish your goals. You have to be your own judge and try to get yourself to do the right thing and stop yourself from doing the wrong thing. Take responsibility for yourself. Only you know your own secrets; no one else can read your mind. If you want to make a change, don't depend on the help of others without taking any initiative yourself.

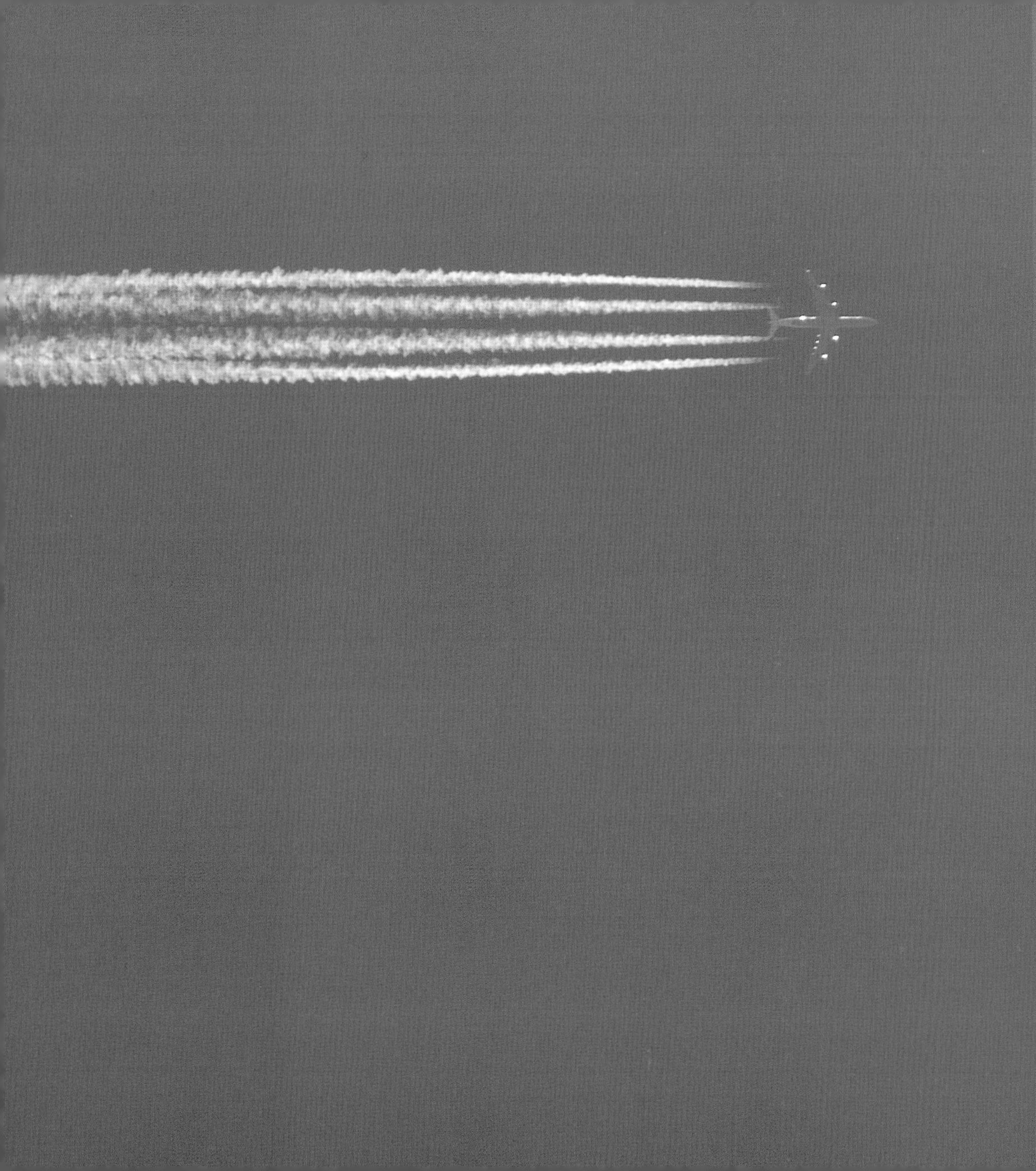

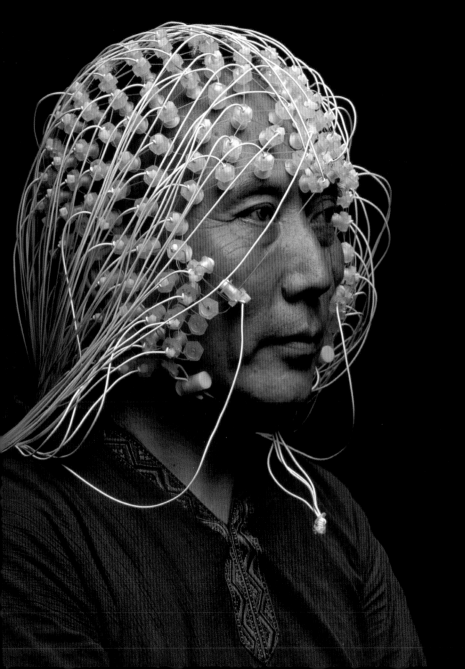

USE YOUR BRAIN

Generally speaking, people are concerned with their own welfare.
You cannot really know whether their advice is meant for your
benefit—or for themselves. You may find some who appear to
want to help you but actually have other intentions and others
who sincerely mean well but lack the wisdom to give good advice.
Taking this into account, it is better to use your own brain and
investigate your situation than to rely on the advice of others.
At least then you will have no regrets.

RIGHT VALUES

Let your actions and words be inspired by values such as honesty and goodwill. This naturally generates mutual trust and affection, which in turn create an atmosphere of peace and harmony. Obstacles in your life will diminish, and you will find it easy to get things done.

FORCE OF TRUTH

To walk the path of truth is difficult. It can even be a bit risky in the beginning. But stick to it and others will gradually realize what is true and you will win their trust. Honesty gives power to your deeds. With dishonesty you may deceive others for a while, but in the end they will lose faith in you and your actions will be ineffective.

STEADY CHARACTER

Everything is impermanent, and it is therefore
natural for each of us to change. Nonetheless,
be more or less consistent in your viewpoint and
behavior. Otherwise, no one will trust you and your
endeavors will be all the more difficult to accomplish.
Try not to be like a feather in the wind!

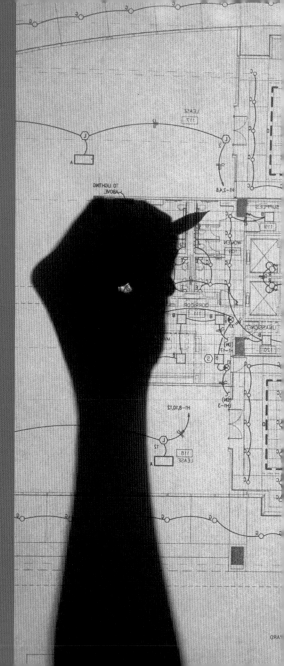

SUCCESS

Hold fast to your aims and accomplish what you set out to achieve. You will be regarded as a capable person. Success comes only if you persistently work at a task and remain totally focused.

RESPECT

Others will respect you only if you are a source of inspiration and they think something good might come from you.

FRIENDS

Although each of us has our own personality, our circle of friends can influence and change us. So it is important to rely on friends who have intelligence and integrity.

KEEP GOOD COMPANY

Are your friends taking you in the right direction? Think about it.
Judge for yourself if their advice is helpful right now, or if it will
lead to something better in the long run. Friends have brought
ruin to many—don't trust them blindly. Discrimination is key.
This doesn't mean that you should totally disregard their advice.
All advice has to be scrutinized. If the outcome is harmful,
so what if it was given with good intentions! Sometimes our
enemies can give the best advice. If it's helpful, take it.

BE LOYAL

Regardless of whether you fall in love or have an arranged marriage, to call someone your companion is a commitment to develop genuine trust and love. Don't be fickle just because of fame or fortune. Despite frustrations and hardships, try to remain loyal until the end. Be caring and supportive. If you give up because of petty ups and downs, it was not a real relationship in the first place.

ISOLATION

Without bonds of mutual trust and affection,
we cannot easily overcome a sense of
loneliness and isolation.

GET INVOLVED

As best you can, try to encourage the good in others and discourage the bad. Don't be indifferent. If you are not able to respond to people's behavior directly, then reckon how to do so in the future. Wait for the right moment. Even if you never have the chance to respond, take stock of what is positive and what is negative. If someone performs a mix of good and bad deeds, respond in whatever way seems most appropriate at the time.

HOW TO JUDGE

To determine what is beneficial or harmful, consider the long-term effects and not just the partial and immediate results. Investigate the context thoroughly and do not be fooled by appearances.

GRATITUDE

Be grateful for all the help that you receive, great or small. With that in mind, try to repay the kindness of others as best you can. If you do so, in the future there will always be more help on the way.

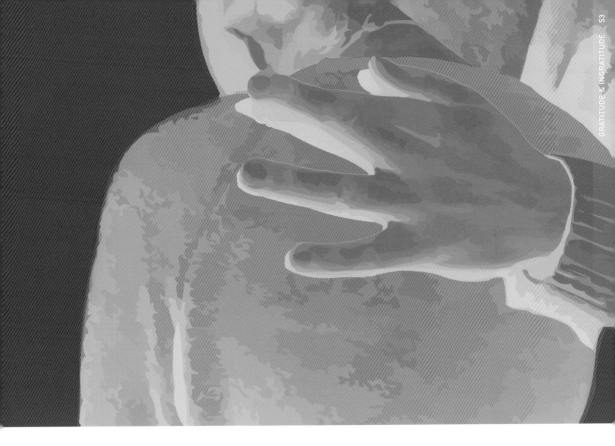

INGRATITUDE

If you not only fail to repay a kindness but also inflict harm on those who help you, then even people who are well-disposed toward you will become discouraged, and all attempts at mutual aid will fail.

THE KINDNESS OF PARENTS

There is nothing like the love of a mother or father. Parents endure great hardships for us and provide everything we need. They raise us and teach us all of life's essentials. Their care and attention cannot be compared with anything else. How ungrateful and callous not to repay their kindness!

MARRIAGE

Marriage is a promise by two people to share their lives together through thick and thin. Whatever comes up, if partners trust and help each other, marriage offers a haven from the tiresome routines of daily life. In troublesome times, you may not always be able to tell if you are friends or foes. But try not to let your marriage get filled with suspicion and spite or it will become an extra burden of misery. Try to stick with it through patience and understanding.

NURTURING A STUDENT

Whether children become good students
depends on their teachers. Occasionally,
a teacher with good intentions and no
self-interest may intimidate and scold
students a bit for their own good.
For the most part, however, a teacher
must be gentle and kind, exposing the
truth of the situation and acknowledging
both faults and positive qualities. Lead
students to subjects of importance and
most of them will take the right path.

TEACHER-STUDENT RELATIONSHIP

The teacher-student relationship depends on two factors. First, how genuinely a teacher guides the student toward a life purpose that matches the student's temperament and intelligence. Second, how genuinely the student follows advice that is advantageous for the future. Lavish gifts and displays of deference are not the point.

SELF-IMPROVEMENT

Many seek to improve themselves,
but few know how to go about it.
Alas, often their efforts are fruitless.
If you want to improve, educate
yourself—learn as much as you can!

KNOWLEDGE

What is important to know? Value knowledge that is most useful right now. Judge knowledge by how effective it is, not by how difficult it is to acquire.

HOBBIES

The more you learn, the more you are able to solve problems and deal with difficult situations. Alongside your main area of focus, why not also study something else just for the fun of it?

EXPERIENCE

To live as equals with others requires a wide range of experience. The wise have much experience and fools have little. To gain experience, you need to go through good and bad times. How can you grow if your experiences are always the same? Anything that happens, good or bad, can be constructive in the end—as long as you learn something useful from it. So when you face difficulties, don't feel too bad!

CRISIS

In a crisis we often find new ways to solve problems.
A crisis can be the source of many creative ideas
and inventions.

SPEAK AND ACT WITH CARE

Think before you speak or act. Otherwise, you may create unnecessary problems. Consider your own abilities, where the situation at hand may be heading, and how your actions and speech will affect other people. If you can clearly see all these factors, then nothing you do or say can cause too much harm.

INVESTIGATION

Investigate the situation properly before taking action, whether in public or in private matters. Consider the long-term implications of your deeds. What is the best way to achieve your aims? What problems might arise and how can you avoid or overcome them? In the face of an insurmountable obstacle, what alternatives exist? The more you tap into your own and other people's experience, the deeper into these questions you can go.

SPEECH

Speak to the point—clearly and lucidly—so that others can hear what you have to say. Tailor your speech to your audience without mixing in your own personal likes and dislikes. Pick gentle words—not too many or too few. Don't omit anything or embellish the facts, and try not to contradict yourself. This is the way to become an effective speaker.

HOW TO SUCCEED

Whatever you have to do, whether
worldly or spiritual in nature,
perform the task with body, speech,
and mind fully engaged. Without
this total involvement nothing will
be accomplished, no matter how
much you think and talk about it.
You can't satisfy hunger unless you
eat. Thinking and talking about
food won't help!

AVOID DISTRACTIONS

In both private and public affairs, to become distracted from your responsibilities is a hindrance to progress. Don't get caught up in side projects. Direct your energy toward immediate responsibilities and single-mindedly carry them out. This way success is assured, because all the right causes for success will be present. There is no fruit without a seed. If you get lost in distractions, you can never accomplish your aims.

STAY FOCUSED

Among your many responsibilities, there is always a main goal. Stay focused on the most important issue. If you choose to pursue many activities at once, you will lag behind in achieving your principal objective.

SINCERE MOTIVATION

In public or private matters, you cannot achieve a goal without sincere motivation. What is sincere motivation? Think to yourself, "I will complete this task in its entirety without deceiving anyone." If you do so, no doubt good results will come from your endeavors.

Make Trade
Clea Green
NO WTO
NO WTO
FREE TRADE
= DEAD
SEA TURTLES
WWW.SEATURTLES.ORG

EARNING OUR KEEP

It is important that each of us earn our keep. If we
don't do something worthwhile in exchange for
our sustenance, we are like parasites.

The All-New
Nissan Xterra

HEALTHY COMPETITION

Everyday activities may be motivated by either competition or external pressure of some kind. Without the need for any encouragement, certain worthy activities naturally ignite a competitive spirit. This competitive spirit can help us to achieve and accomplish good things.

ASPIRE TO GREATNESS

If we are attached to petty concerns and never aspire to anything great, we won't accomplish much. What is petty and what is great? Petty is for oneself alone, for immediate gratification, and for harmful deeds, while great is for the many, for the long term, and for positive pursuits. Look closely—what have you or those around you achieved? Avoid pettiness and aspire to great things!

TAKE ACTION

Investigate the consequences of your action. What are the pros and cons? Is your action really beneficial or harmful? Once you have investigated, make your decision—and act! Without taking action, your thoughts remain thoughts, and you cannot accomplish anything.

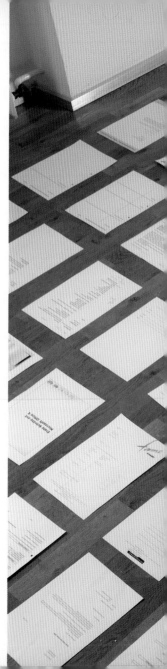

REVISE PLANS

As you work toward your objective, try to incorporate good ideas and abandon bad ones. Otherwise, you cannot accomplish the task properly.

INFORMED DECISIONS

When taking on a new project, no one can avoid making decisions. What to include? What to discard? Decide only after thorough consideration, weighing the benefits and drawbacks for both the short and the long term. How foolish to base your decisions on the whims of others!

PROJECTS

It is impossible to pursue all of your ideas.
Take on only those projects that you are able
to accomplish. Life will be less troublesome.

CONTENTMENT

The more we pursue sensual pleasures, the more we crave them and chase after distractions. Our dissatisfaction increases and creates mental stress and physical discomfort. Recognize how this happens, and learn to be content with a few necessities. You will be more carefree and joyful.

MODERN CONVENIENCES

Even though amenities are meant to make life easier and more comfortable, watch out! Rely on them too much without setting limits and suffering soon follows.

WEALTH

Wealth can be a source of both happiness and misery.
To accumulate wealth is fine—so long as you
know how to use it properly.

A GRAVE MISTAKE

To risk your own life for the sake of money is a grave mistake. It is like cutting the tree's roots in order to save its branches.

MISTAKEN APPROACH

Harming anyone—yourself or others—to gain happiness is like eating poison to prolong life. It is a mistaken approach and you will not achieve what you are seeking.

BLIND FAITH

To trust something without seeing clearly
whether it is beneficial or not is blind faith.
It hampers the development of wisdom.

RECOGNIZE YOUR MISTAKES

For human beings, it is impossible not to make mistakes. If you recognize mistakes on your own or through feedback from others, you can take steps to correct them and minimize the damage. But if you cling to your errors as if they were inviolable truths, you will not achieve your greater purpose.

TO PREVENT NEGATIVE DEEDS

Promise yourself that you will never do anything that will bring disgrace to your community. This resolve will prevent you from engaging in destructive behavior.

COOPERATION

Cooperation is based on mutual appreciation and dependence. No common objective can be realized without it. To foster an environment of cooperation, take mutual benefit and mutual agreement as your main goal. Be prepared to adopt good ideas and discard harmful ones regardless of where they may come from. Look far into the future with an open and accommodating mind.

DISCORD

Suppose you set out to incite discord as a means to some end of your own. You may succeed, bringing misery to everyone—yourself included! But eventually, your intentions will be discovered. You will lose the trust of others and with it your authority and ability to be of influence. So much for your success! In the final analysis, you are the real loser.

SUPERIOR POINTS OF VIEW

You may have more or less understanding of how
to benefit society depending on your intelligence,
but don't cling too fiercely to the superiority
of your own ideas and views. If you do, you will
create barriers to social harmony and cooperation.

CONFLICT

Conflict is a natural aspect of human life. It's just not possible to be completely free of it. But since it makes all sides involved miserable, try to minimize disagreements and refrain from stirring things up.

CONSISTENCY

There is no one who does not change. Life is a sequence
of different thoughts, emotions, and activities. You cannot
fully trust yourself not to change, let alone anyone else.
Recognizing this, you can see that reliability is just
a matter of degree.

VIRTUES AND VICES

Over the course of our lives, we acquire both virtues and vices depending on various causes and circumstances. No one can remain on a steady course, sticking consistently to only virtue or vice. Everyone's life is a mix. You cannot accurately judge others by one or two deeds, good or bad!

THINGS CHANGE

It is impossible to be at your best or your worst at all times. Who is always consistent? Everyone changes according to different situations and as they go through life's different phases. There is no point in feeling great pride or great shame simply because of temporary circumstances.

FREEDOM AND PROGRESS

For humans to advance further, we must assure
freedom of speech and action. Our intelligence
increases the more we engage in activity. Freedom
of speech and action propels us into new areas
of knowledge and innovation. Scientific and
technological discoveries are not possible if not
for the freedom to experiment. Without freedom
a human being is like a caged animal.

FREEDOM WITH SELF-RESTRAINT

Freedom is the foundation for happiness. It allows you to choose pursuits according to your own interests. But with freedom, exercise self-restraint. Without it, you are likely to become discontented and self-destructive. Why? Because desires have no limits!

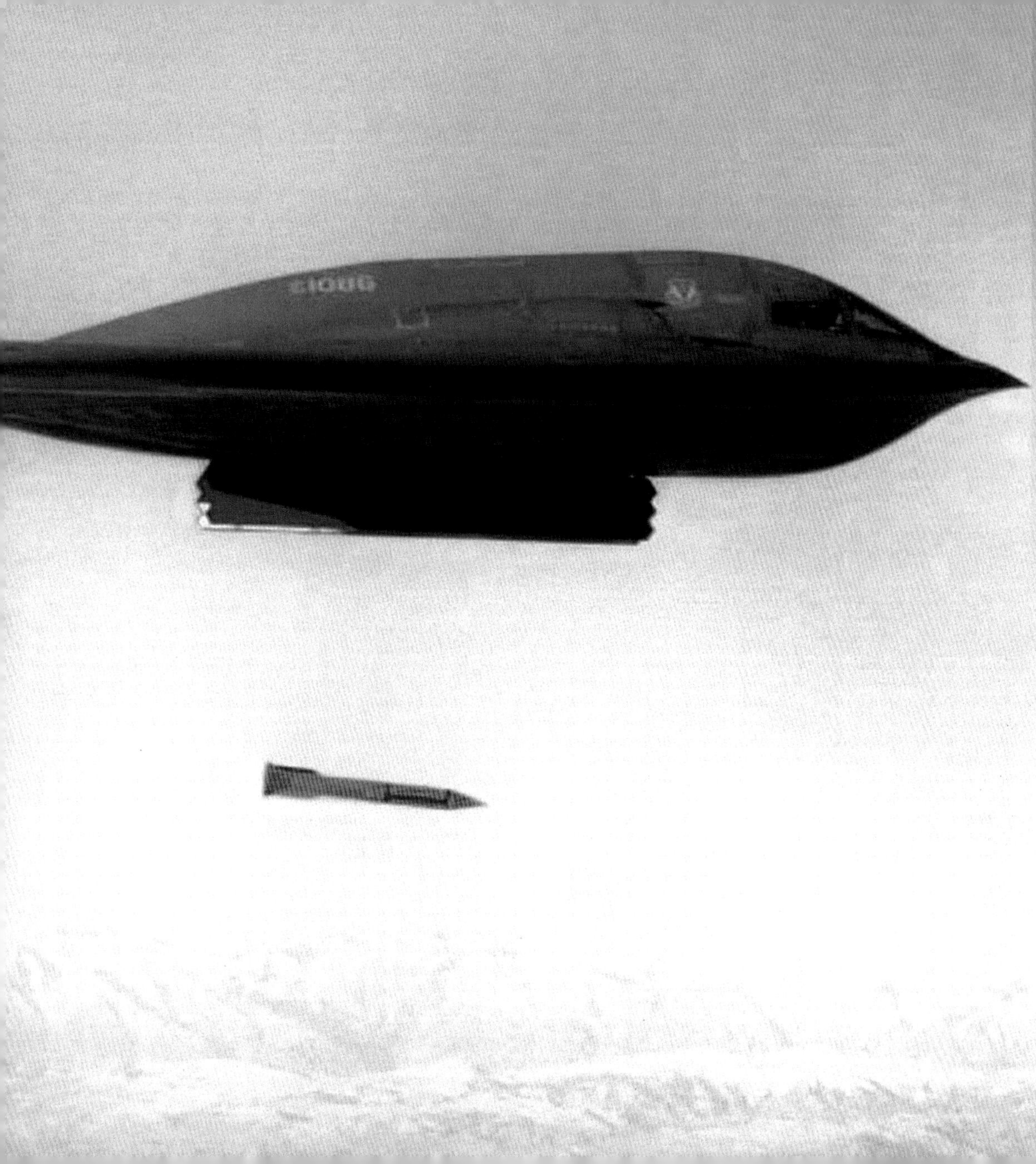

COMFORT

Abundance can create the conditions
for a good life, but too much luxury will
not increase your happiness. In excess,
it is like eating a big meal just after
finishing one. What's the point? The best
way to find happiness is to gain more
freedom—even if it means less comfort.

TRUE PEACE

True peace cannot be achieved by force or by merely
invoking the word "peace." It can only be attained by
training the mind and learning to cultivate inner peace.
Peace is a calm and gentle state of mind.

TIBETAN

As languages are all useful for communicating, no language is better or worse than any other. Nonetheless, some languages are valued over others because of the wisdom they convey and preserve. If you seek to cultivate the art of happiness, for example, Tibetan is very useful.

BE IN SYNC

Each of us has the right to our own opinions and views.
But unless you want to be totally isolated, adjust your
perspective from time to time so that you are in sync
with the society around you. If you must have your
own way all the time, you will never be able to live
in harmony with others.

GET TO THE POINT

If the main objective at hand is achieved, the process is
not so important. Don't be too fussy about the details.
It is difficult to satisfy everybody because each
person has a different opinion.

THE COMMON INTEREST

Try to serve the common interest. Whatever happens, think about what is best for the group rather than acting for yourself alone. The benefit of many is more important than that of each individual. If you cannot tell the difference, there is no way you can serve the public. What's more, your own interests will be ill served.

A BETTER FUTURE

Our hope for a better future places a heavy responsibility
on the younger generation. How to meet this challenge?
Try to educate yourself in areas that will benefit society.
Take up spiritual disciplines that open your heart and mind.
Cooperate with others and establish harmonious relations
with all people regardless of ethnicity, gender, or age.
Do everything you can to stop the misuse of our natural
resources and the senseless destruction of our environment.
With ethical discernment, you—the youth of today—can
create prosperity for the world and humankind. Otherwise,
our future is bleak.

THE ENVIRONMENT

The environment is irreplaceable. All life forms on earth coexist
in delicate balance. Although some habitats are naturally more
abundant than others, we are degrading the environment by
exploiting and polluting it, affecting the entire world irrespective
of borders. For everyone's sake, let's stop polluting the environment.
How foolish to destroy our planet—which has to sustain present and
future generations. Together, let's protect and safeguard the earth.

POLLUTION

It's not as if the environment pollutes itself or pollution comes from natural calamities over which we have no control. A contaminated environment is the result of human greed. In the final analysis, the fate of the environment is entirely in our hands.

FUTURE DANGER

Governments and private enterprise are
relentlessly destroying the environment for
the sake of some temporary economic gain.
This presents a grave danger for the future.
If we don't intervene, the world will become
a desolate place.

A COMMON ENEMY

Excessive mining, pesticide use, and excavation ravage the environment in ways that can never be reversed. Whoever engages in this devastation is the common enemy of all countries and people and passes on an enormous burden of suffering to future generations.

COMMON SENSE

Whatever is good or bad for you is likely to be so for others. If you want to get along with people, apply your own experience and give others what they need. Use your common sense to live more harmoniously with others!

THE POWER OF EMPATHY

We all react in similar ways to what is pleasant and what is unpleasant. Understanding this, we know how to help each other. Why not support others in promoting goodness and preventing harm?

HELP EACH OTHER

Everything is interdependent. No one is entirely self-sufficient. We rely on human society for mutual support. Harm someone and you weaken your own support system. Why cause harm to yourself? Instead, try to help others as much as possible.

PROTECT THE HUMAN RACE

We are capable of having a huge impact on
the world. The only way for us to protect
our species—and the planet—from our
own destructive power is to do everything
possible to maintain peace and stability
among ourselves. Therefore, it is
worthwhile for all of us to study and
lovingly preserve all the religions,
traditions, and systems that promote
peace and unity for humankind.

PROTECT ANIMALS

Animals react to pain and pleasure just as we do. We enjoy their company as companions and friends, and they are indispensable to the planet's ecosystem. Do whatever you can to prevent the extinction of any animal species. After all, future generations will hold us accountable.

THE LAW

Laws to prohibit negative deeds result from people's misconduct. These punitive laws can only be effective if, first and foremost, those who make them abide by them.

MAR. 3 1991

THE MILITARY

The purpose of the military is to protect peace and stability, not just to kill the enemy. Imagine how wonderful it would be if our military also learned methods for cultivating inner peace and joy.

FAME

Celebrities in all fields of endeavor can use their fame
and accomplishments for the benefit of assisting
others and help the world become a better place.

IGNORANCE

To conclude that something is good or bad without proper reasons is a sign of ignorance.

HOW TO CHOOSE

How do you decide whether or not to do something? Ask yourself how much benefit the activity is likely to bring.

EXPECTATIONS

It's okay for people to expect things from you,
but you have the right to refuse if need be.
There is no shame in that.

PRIVILEGES AND OBLIGATIONS

If you enjoy a special position or certain privileges,
you might have to assume corresponding obligations.
Be aware of this. Don't shirk your responsibilities.

SELFISHNESS

Everyone is searching for love and support. But few are prepared to actually give love and support to others.

A GREAT BEING

Someone who is totally dedicated to
the benefit of others is truly a great
and marvelous being. Such a person's
actions and intentions far surpass
those of ordinary humans.

HARD TO HELP, EASY TO HARM

It is quite difficult for us to help ourselves,
let alone others. At the same time, it is all
too easy to cause harm. Sometimes it seems
as if we are all trying to harm each other.

LONELINESS

Cheat and harm others for selfish ends and you will lose their love and trust. What happens then? Without love and trust, you experience loneliness—whether you live on your own or in the midst of others. Imagine no one with whom to share the joys and sorrows of life. Imagine no one to rely on, no one to turn to for help or confide in, and no one to love. Tormented and anguished, a lonely person cares not whether he lives or dies.

INTOXICATION

Some get intoxicated in order to have a good time.
Watch out! Intoxication can hinder your future
prospects and generally affect your health and
well-being. It produces exactly the opposite
of what you are seeking.

LIGHTEN UP

Who knows what you will see, hear, or experience in these chaotic and turbulent times? Try to protect yourself from becoming too overwhelmed by pain and suffering. Lighten up! Don't take things so seriously. With a broad and accommodating mind, you can keep a sense of perspective.

INTERDEPENDENCE

Everything is interdependent. Pleasant and unpleasant experiences occur because of many causes and conditions. Nothing in life has a single or independent cause. Therefore, it makes no sense to attribute your joy or anger to one person or thing as the sole source of your pleasure or unhappiness.

PEOPLE

Alas, look!

What is more restless than a human being?

No one wants trouble,

yet most problems in life are man-made.

One day, if we stop being so busy,

no doubt the world will become

a peaceful place to live.

A PRAYER FOR PEACE

I always pray for true peace, joy, and harmony in this world. But it is a difficult aspiration to realize. So long as there is envy and rivalry, violence cannot be stopped. Unless violence ends, there is no way for my prayer to be answered.

PRISONERS

Though our eyes are intelligent enough
to see the shape of good and evil,
inevitably, we seize the opposite of what we seek.
Relinquishing freedom,
we become prisoners of our own afflictions.

MIND

Although mind is not a physical substance and is experienced as something other than matter, it nevertheless has a profound connection to the body. The body affects the mind and the mind also affects the body. To improve your state of mind, keep your body healthy and train your mind to cultivate peace and tranquility, using the teachings of authentic traditions. If you take care in your conduct and maintain an expansive outlook, then regardless of life's ups and downs, you will feel more at ease.

BUDDHISM

The essence of Buddhism is to discover a state of lasting happiness and to work for the benefit of others. On this path, wisdom and compassion are inseparable. Little by little, through a process of investigation, we gradually come closer to understanding the truth.

THE BENEFITS OF DHARMA

The benefits of dharma recounted by the Buddha and his disciples are the results of the proper practice of dharma. You cannot reap all those benefits just by listening to a few teachings. If you do not practice, you will think that the dharma does not work—especially when problems arise and you cannot deal with them. You might even give up the dharma and never benefit from it. To enjoy its positive effects, practice it first.

A GENUINE MONK

A genuine monk should have devotion to Buddha, Dharma, and Sangha; confidence in the law of karma; sincerity in following the Buddhist teachings; and compassion for all beings. Monks lacking in any of these qualities are monks in name only. In fact, they are impostors and deceive their devoted followers.

RELIGION

Assess a religion on the basis of its teachings.
The deeds of its followers are a different matter;
whether good or bad, they belong to individuals
and not to the teachings. Don't mix up the two.

THE ROOT OF HAPPINESS

Discover which actions truly produce happiness
and which result in suffering. Using discernment,
take up what brings benefit and discard what
causes harm. Live accordingly and you'll be on

THE RIGHT DIRECTION

Take responsibility for creating and promoting
situations that benefit society. Likewise, try
to eliminate and uproot situations that
harm others. This is the duty of each
and every one of us and paves
the way to a better future.

A SHARED PURPOSE

People have different characters, interests, and opinions because of their life circumstances and backgrounds. Nevertheless, let us work together toward a shared purpose—to eliminate suffering and achieve happiness.

PAST, PRESENT, AND FUTURE

Don't hold on to the past. Let go of feelings of joy or anger toward whatever has happened, good or bad. The past is already over. Pay attention to the present so you can create the future you seek. This is a meaningful way to live.

EVERYDAY FALLACIES

Fame and fortune are but rainbows in the sky.
Loved ones—friends and family—are mere etchings on water.
The business of living life is simply last night's dream.
All creation is just a flash of lightning in the dark.

BIRTH AND DEATH

Nurtured by my mother's love and warmth,
I stepped anew into this human world.
Its limitless and ever-changing marvels
I pursued with a restless, grasping mind,
tasting joy, sorrow, laughter, and anguish.
At the end of my days, once again,
I must pass into a state of dissolution.
This is the nature of the world of samsara.

A SHORT BIOGRAPHY OF HIS HOLINESS THE 17TH GYALWANG KARMAPA

by Khenpo Gawang of Kyodrak

I humbly bow down to the Three Jewels.
I take refuge in them.
May I receive their blessings.

His Holiness the Seventeenth Gyalwang Karmapa, Ogyen Trinley Dorje, is the spiritual head of the Karma Kagyu school of Tibetan Buddhism and a living emanation of Chenrezig, the Buddha of Compassion.

The Karmapas are Tibet's great wisdom teachers, the oldest lineage in Tibetan Buddhism, going back to the 11th century, and the first to introduce the practice of identifiable reincarnation. Traditionally, the Karmapa would identify his successor by means of a "prediction letter," written shortly before his death, foretelling exactly where his next incarnation would be found.

It was just such a letter, written by His Holiness the Sixteenth Gyalwang Karmapa, who had died in 1981, that led a search party to the home of a nomadic family in eastern Tibet, where an eight-year-old boy named Apo Gaga was identified as the true reincarnation of the Karmapa.

Apo Gaga—or Karmapa Ogyen Trinley Dorje, as he would be renamed on his enthronement—was born in Bakor, Lhadok, in the province of Kham in eastern Tibet. It is a nomadic area surrounded by mountains. The Dzachu River flows in the east and the Drichu River flows in the west. The hills and valleys are green pastureland, and flowers of all colors fill the meadows in the summer. You feel that you have arrived in heaven.

The people of Kham are warriors, known for their hardy disposition, boisterous good humor, and rough-and-ready manners. But what they lack in politeness they make up for in honesty and their unswerving faith in the Buddhist teachings of kindness and compassion. They respect the monks and elders. Their lives may be hard, but they have a deep tradition of helping others in need.

H.H. THE SIXTEENTH GYALWANG KARMAPA, RANGJUNG RIGPE DORJE.

LHADOK, KHAM.

OPPOSITE: THE SEVENTEENTH KARMAPA, AGE SEVEN.

THE KARMAPA'S FATHER, KARMA THONDUP.

THE KARMAPA'S MOTHER, LOGA.

The Karmapa was born on the first day of the fifth month of the Tibetan calendar, June 19, 1985, at daybreak. It is not uncommon in Tibet for the births of great lamas to be attended by all manner of signs and wonders, and so it was with the Karmapa. It is said that many rainbows appeared above the tent where he was born, birds sang in a heavenly chorus, and the sound of a conch shell could be heard throughout the valley—a propitious omen—although no one could be found blowing such a shell and no conch shell had ever sounded as loud as this one. From that moment on, local people showed the boy special reverence as they knew that he was a reincarnation of a great being, although at that time he had not been recognized as the reincarnation of the Karmapa. His older sister named him Apo Gaga, or "happy brother."

His father, Karma Thondup, and his mother, Loga, were good people, much loved and respected by others. There were six daughters and three sons in the family, including Apo Gaga. The family herded sheep, goats, and yaks; in the summer months, when they drove their animals to the good pastures for grazing, they lived in a tent made of yak hair. In the winter, when the snows made grazing impossible, the family lived in a sturdy wooden hut that Karma Thondup built.

The family were devout Buddhists. The centerpiece of their home was a shrine with a small statue of the Buddha, with butter lamps and offering bowls. On the shrine was a photograph of the Sixteenth Karmapa, Rangjung Rigpe Dorje, with whom Karma Thondup had a strong connection. When Karma Thondup was young, his parents had taken him to see the Karmapa, who was visiting Kham, and it was the Karmapa who had actually given Karma Thondup his name.

Life was hard for the family; the only thing not scarce was love. When Apo Gaga was very young, his mother gave him a bowl of rice cooked in milk. He remembers that bowl of rice as the most delicious food that he has ever eaten, and he talks of it still. His main playmate was a big and strong billy goat with a white patch and white stripes and a colorful tassle on his right ear. This goat was very wild and no one else could catch it, but it meekly followed Apo Gaga everywhere.

So it was that time passed until Apo Gaga's eighth year. At that time, a search party from the Karmapas' ancestral monastery of Tsurphu, in central Tibet, came to the family's home, following the instructions laid out in the prediction letter of the Sixteenth Karmapa. Apo Gaga was recognized as the true and only reincarnation of the Sixteenth Karmapa, Rangjung Rigpe Dorje. His Holiness the Dalai Lama, taking into consideration the supporting documents and his own dream indicating the place of the current reincarnation's birth, officially recognized the boy as the Seventeenth Karmapa. On Saga Dawa, the full moon day of the fourth month of the Tibetan calendar, which marks the Buddha's birthday, enlightenment, and death—June 17, 1992—the Karmapa arrived at Tsurphu. There, on September 27, 1992, he was enthroned in high ceremony by two of the "heart sons" of the previous Karmapa, Their Eminences Situ Rinpoche and Gyaltsab Rinpoche. At the same time, a representative of the People's Republic of China announced the government's formal recognition of the Karmapa, declaring that this was the first time that China had recognized a reincarnation of a lama.

Representatives from monasteries of all schools of Tibetan Buddhism, along with some 50,000 devotees from 34 countries, gathered at this

THE KARMAPA ARRIVING AT TSURPHU MONASTERY, 1992.

THE KARMAPA WEARING A CEREMONIAL BLACK HAT.

THE KARMAPA WITH H.E. SITU RINPOCHE.

H.E. GYALTSAB RINPOCHE.

OPPOSITE: THE KARMAPA, 1992.

remote monastery to participate in the ceremony and to be present as the Karmapa gave his first empowerment of Chenrezig, the Lord of Compassion.

In 1994, the Karmapa was invited to visit China for a pilgrimage to holy places. That September, after paying homage and offering prayers at the Potala Palace—the ancestral home of the dalai lamas—and the Jokhang Temple, he set out for Beijing. There he was welcomed at a reception by the Chinese president, Jiang Zemin.

The great importance that the Chinese authorities accorded him during this tour began to raise fears in the Karmapa's mind that they had intentions of using him against the Dalai Lama and the true cause of the Tibetan people. These fears increased when his repeated requests to visit his teachers in India and elsewhere, to receive the teachings and instruction necessary for his spiritual development, were denied.

"I was afraid that the Chinese might force me to accept a complicated and high-sounding position. I would become a disgrace to the Tibetan race if I had to do something that would harm the true cause of Tibet and if I had to oppose the Dalai Lama," he later said.

It was for this reason that in 1999, at the age of 14, the Karmapa made his momentous decision to escape to India. "The most important and primary reason for me to escape was to receive teachings from H.H. the Dalai Lama and other great lamas such as Situ Rinpoche and Gyaltsab Rinpoche," he explained. "To meet my devoted students in foreign countries and to visit Rumtek Monastery, the seat of the Sixteenth Karmapa, were the secondary reasons."

He confided his decision to Lama Nyima, his tutor, and asked him to make all possible arrangements for his escape. By now the Karmapa was unable to leave Tsurphu without permission from the government, and his movements within the monastery were closely watched by officials. Following Lama Nyima's plan, the Karmapa told the monastery authorities that on the night of December 28 he would be going into a solitary meditative retreat in his rooms. There he was joined by his attendant Zimpon Drupnam. For the first time since his recognition, the Karmapa dispensed with his monk's robes, disguising himself in a workman's trousers and jacket. A woolen scarf was wrapped around his neck and a hat pulled down tightly over his ears.

When Zimpon Drupnam asked what precious things they needed to carry with them, the Karmapa told him, "We are risking our lives for the sake of teachings and to benefit beings. We do not need to get attached to any material things. We will not bring anything valuable with us." They left with nothing except what they needed for the road.

The Karmapa prayed to the Three Jewels and invoked the help of Dharma Protectors to make his mission successful. Then he and Zimpon Drupnam climbed out of the window and made their escape. Beyond the monastery walls, a jeep was waiting. At 10:30 P.M. local time, in a group of five people, both monks and laity, the Karmapa drove away from Tsurphu for the last time.

Fearing that they would be followed, they broke the taillights of the jeep and drove on, the night enveloping them like a shroud. As fast as they drove, it seemed to them as if the car was stuck on the road and that the road was stretching before them like an elastic band. They frequently

THE KARMAPA (CENTER) DURING THE ESCAPE.

THE KARMAPA (LEFT) AT THE NEPALESE BORDER.

OPPOSITE: TSURPHU MONASTERY.

The Karmapa on horseback.

First meeting with H.H. the Dalai Lama, Dharamsala.

lost their way in the darkness, and they were constantly afraid that they would be stopped.

At length they came to a military camp on the road. Fearing discovery, the Karmapa and two of the party left the car and set off into the hills to walk around the camp, with the intention of rejoining the car further down the road on the other side. As they could not use flashlights and there was no moon in the sky, the climb was dangerous, and they tripped over rocks and tore their hands on thorns. But when at last they reached the road on the other side of the camp, there was no sign of the car, and it took a long while for the two parties to meet. Each feared that the other had been caught. It was one of the most difficult times and everyone said their hearts were in their mouths. After that, they had to pass more than one checkpoint, and each time it was as if they were criminals on the run from the law. It was their good fortune that it was the coldest time of the year and the guards were sheltering in their barracks. On December 30, they finally arrived at the Nepalese border near Loyul, worried, frightened, and tired.

They had made good their escape, but still they were a long way from freedom. The road had come to an end, and they had to abandon the jeep. From there on they traveled on horseback and on foot.

They had to climb high mountains and steep gorges and navigate passes so narrow that even the birds feared to fly through them. On some paths they had to crawl on all fours, and the slightest loss of balance would have plunged them hundreds of feet down into the gorge below. They had to cross the snow mountain where the snow never melted. The high altitude made it hard to breathe and the wind cut into their flesh like a sharp knife. There were blinding blizzards and landslides and rolling stones coming down like hailstorms, threatening to trap them or to knock them off balance and sweep them off the side of the mountain to certain death. They traveled by day and by night, with no time to stop and rest. All were fighting for their breath; no one could talk, and food had no taste. Their bodies grew weak, exhausted, and sick with the change of climate and altitude. The Karmapa had injured his back and pains shot through his stomach. He felt profound fatigue and sadness, but his courage never faltered. On January 2, 2000, they came to a lodge. There they were able to hire a helicopter to fly to Yambu. That same night they hired a taxi and crossed the border into Indian territory. They took a train to Lucknow, then went on to Delhi by taxi and from Delhi on to Dharamsala, the seat of the Tibetan government in exile. There, on January 5, the Karmapa was received by His Holiness the Dalai Lama.

The exhaustion of body and mind, the fears and difficulties of the journey, the joy of accomplishing the desired goal of arriving under the protection of the Dalai Lama, the abundance of love and affection bestowed on him by His Holiness, his wise counsel and melodious voice—all of this gave the Karmapa such an astounding feeling that he could neither cry nor laugh. All of his anxieties were now gone, as if an enormous burden had been taken from his back. The Dalai Lama and the Tibetan government gave him the warmest welcome. The Tibetan community in exile and the Himalayan Buddhists greeted him with unimaginable joy and devotion. The whole world was enthralled by his escape. While mindful of the political sensitivities involved, the Indian government also offered its protection.

AFTER THE FIRST MEETING WITH H.H. THE DALAI LAMA.

THE KARMAPA WITH THE TIBETAN GOVERNMENT IN EXILE.

THE KARMAPA WITH H.H. THE DALAI LAMA IN
BODHGAYA, 2003.

WITH HIS TEACHER VEN. KENCHEN
THRANGU RINPOCHE.

OPPOSITE: THE KARMAPA PRESIDING OVER A
PRAYER CEREMONY FESTIVAL, 2006.

The Karmapa and his party took up residence at Gyuto Tantric Monastery, which had been newly built in the village of Sidhbari in the Kangra Valley near Dharamsala. He was joyfully reunited with his teachers H.E. Situ Rinpoche and H.E. Gyaltsab Rinpoche and started to receive teachings from them and other lamas as well. All his wishes in coming to India began to be fulfilled.

In March 2001 the Karmapa traveled for the first time to Bodhgaya, where the Lord Buddha attained enlightenment, and visited many holy sites nearby. The next month he gave his first press conference. More than 100 journalists from news media all over the world, including the BBC and CNN, gathered in Dharamsala. Speaking with great self-assurance, dignity, and precision, the 15-year-old Karmapa answered a range of questions on his escape, his feelings about the Tibetan cause and the Dalai Lama, his everyday routine, and his plans for the future. All who were present were impressed by the Karmapa's great composure and his air of authority. One journalist later wrote that when the media arrived in Dharamsala, they all had one question at the top of their lists: "Are you the true Karmapa?" At the press conference, nobody asked that question because no one felt the need to.

In 2008, the Karmapa left India for the first time to visit America. The visits by his predecessor, the Sixteenth Karmapa, during the 1970s and 1980s had been historic occasions for the Western Buddhist community and had led to the founding of the Karmapa's seat in America, Karma Triyana Dharmachakra Monastery in Woodstock, New York. For the Karmapa finally to set foot in America eight years after his escape was cause for great rejoicing. In May he arrived in New York, where he gave dharma teachings to large gatherings of people. From there he moved on

to Boulder and Seattle. Wherever he went, people were greatly inspired by his presence and the quality of his teachings and hopeful that this visit would set a precedent for the Karmapa to travel throughout the world spreading the Buddha-dharma.

The Karmapa continues to live at Gyuto, where his time is devoted to the study and practice of Buddhism. In his spare moments he loves to write poetry, and he enjoys painting and music. He has a great love for animals and nature, and he has a particular interest in the environment. In his public talks he has spoken often of the need for everyone to take responsibility for their own actions in protecting the environment and to be mindful of their place in their world and their relations to others.

"For the human race, there are two conditions in this world that can make us advance," he says. "The first condition is to go forward out of fear. All beings, including animals, will advance out of fear. They sense a danger to their existence, feel fear and terror, and find a way to remedy their situation. But moving forward because you see a benefit or profit is probably something that mainly we humans do. We are beings with brains and intelligence. But if we simply exist, without doing anything meaningful, then we simply become another mouth to feed, another person using up space, another body crowding the world, and there is no benefit at all.

"While living in the world, we need to demonstrate intelligence and define our vision for the future. Only then will our existence in the world be meaningful and will we be able to benefit the other creatures who live with us on this earth."

THE KARMAPA TEACHING IN SEATTLE, 2008.

OPPOSITE: THE KARMAPA IN BOULDER, 2008.

THE KARMAPA IN BODHGAYA.

OPPOSITE: THE KARMAPA ARRIVING AT KARMA TRIYANA DHARMACHAKRA MONASTERY, WOODSTOCK, NEW YORK, 2008.

NEXT PAGE: GYUTO TANTRIC MONASTERY.

At this time the Karmapa is nearly six feet tall. His features are well balanced. He has a booming, melodious voice and is sparing with his words, saying only what is necessary, and with deep meaning. He has a very kind and considerate personality. He does not have the pride of even an ordinary monk. He seems to have very little attachment to his name and fame and gives honesty and truth a very high value. He has a broad mind and can accommodate both good and bad people and occurrences with equanimity. He considers all sides of a question before making any decisions. He treats every person equally, making no distinction between those of high and low status. It is difficult to come close to him, but once you are close he always treats you like a friend and does not change. He is already very learned, and if he continues to study as he is doing now, there is every indication that he will become a great scholar.

This is a brief but true story.
There is no tale of gods and ghosts.
There is no story of victory and conquest.
It is just the record of what really happened.

As His Holiness the Karmapa and my friend Ringu Tulku asked me to write a short biography of the present Karmapa for his book, *The Future Is Now*, I have just put down some of the events in the life of His Holiness as I have heard from him and others near him without any alteration.

Khenpo Gawang of Kyodrak.

Written on the twenty-sixth day of the eighth month of Earth Mouse year, seventeenth Rabjung (September 25, 2008)

Jayantu

ACKNOWLEDGMENTS

This book is based on my teachings and occasional reflections. I would like to express my appreciation to Gordon Campbell who repeatedly encouraged me to offer something like this for readers everywhere, especially keeping in mind the youth of today; to Khenpo Gawang of Kyodak who assisted me in selecting and editing the sayings; and to Ringu Tulku who volunteered to translate the text into English. I thank them all sincerely.

The Seventeenth Karmapa, Ogyen Trinley Dorje

Gordon Campbell of the Academy of Everything is Possible is deeply indebted to His Holiness the Seventeenth Gyalwang Karmapa for his kindness and generosity. He thanks all those whose invaluable assistance and support made this project possible: His Holiness the Dalai Lama, Ven. Ringu Tulku Rinpoche, Ven. Dilyak Drupon Rinpoche, Khenpo Gawang, Ngodup Tsering Burkhar, Paul O'Connor, Paula Litzky, Patricia Gift, Mick Brown, Holly Gayley, Matthieu Ricard, Robert A.F. Thurman, Karmapa Foundation, Karma Triyana Dharmachakra, Rüdiger Findeisen, Andrew Firman, Lynn C. Franklin, Robert and Lauren Hensey, Rebecca Jobson, Michelle Kelly, Satish Kumar, Paul K., Peter Lamborn Wilson, Gaby Naher, Bernice Paolozzi, Gordon Ryan, Bipin Shah, True Sims, and the monks of Gyuto Tantric Monastery. He also thanks all those who took part in the interview in Dharamsala: Nana Ayim, Chantal Fortune, Charlotte Fraser, Naomi Kirwan, Francesca Marks, Alexandra McGuinness, Joseph Parmet, Jasper Reynolds, Cha Cha Seigne, Ananta Kr. Shrestha, and Robbie Stiefel.

IMAGE CREDITS

The publisher thanks the photographers and organizations for their kind permission to reproduce the following photographs in this book.

Cover James Gritz / © Karmapa Foundation. **v-vii** Paul O'Connor. **3** Aman Sharma / AP / PA Photos. **5** James Gritz / © Karmapa Foundation. **7-8** Paul O'Connor. **11** Robin Bartholick / Getty Images. **12** Clemens Kuby. **14** Columbine High School Shooting, Second Anniversary Memorial Service, Littleton, Colorado, April 20, 2001. Michael Smith / Getty Images. **17** Paul O'Connor. **19** Beverly Joubert / National Geographic / Getty Images. **21** Paul O'Connor. **23** Paul Chesley / Getty Images. **24** Brad Wilson / Getty Images. **27** Paul O'Connor. **28** Cary Wolinsky / Getty Images. **31** Didier Robcis / Getty Images. **33** Peter H. Sprosty / Getty Images. **35** Paul McCormick / Getty Images. **37** Terry Vine / Getty Images. **38** Karen Moskowitz / Getty Images. **41** Karan Kapoor / Getty Images. **42** Masaaki Toyoura / Getty Images. **45** Chris Windsor / Getty Images. **47** Paul O'Connor. **48** Frank Barrett / Getty Images. **52-53** Paul O'Connor. **55** Gen Nishino / Getty Images. **56** Phillip Underdown / Getty Images. **59** CMSP / Getty Images. **60** Paul O'Connor. **63** Tim Hall / Getty Images. **65** Steve Taylor / Getty Images. **66** Lori Adamski-Peek / Getty Images. **69** Mike Powell / Getty Images. **71** Russell Illig / Getty Images. **73** Ray Massey / Getty Images. **75** JFB / Getty Images. **77** Paul Gilham / Getty Images. **79** Paul O'Connor. **80** Leland Bobbe / Getty Images. **83** Paul O'Connor. **85** Daniel Sheehan / Getty Images. **87** Tim Flach / Getty Images. **88** Fernando Leon / Getty Images. **91** Scott Sroka / National Geographic / Getty Images. **92** Paul O'Connor. **95** Christian Hoehn / Getty Images. **96** Absodels / Getty Images. **98** Nicholas Rigg / Getty Images. **101** Steve Cole / Getty Images. **102** Getty Images. **104** David Malan / Getty Images. **107** Sandro Miller / Getty Images. **108** Yuri Cortez / AFP / Getty Images. **111** Loungepark / Getty Images. **113** Pnc / Getty Images. **114** Christopher Furlong / Getty Images. **116** Dennis O'Clair / Getty Images. **119** Ray Pietro / Getty Images. **121** D. Falconer / PhotoLink / Getty Images. **122** Colorblind / Getty Images. **125** Paul O'Connor. **126** Noel Hendrickson / Getty Images. **129** John Knill / Getty Images. **130** Time & Life Pictures / Getty Images. **133** USAF / Getty Images. **134** Poncho / Getty Images. **137** Emmanuel Faure / Getty Images. **138** China Tourism Press / Getty Images. **141** Stephanie Rausser / Getty Images. **142** Julie Toy / Getty Images. **145** Kelvin Murray / Getty Images. **146** David McNew / Getty Images. **149** Mitch Epstein / Getty Images. **150** Marco Polo / Getty Images. **153** Paul O'Connor. **155** Grant Faint / Getty Images. **157** Betsie Van der Meer / Getty Images. **158** Nadia Mackenzie / Getty Images. **161** Martin Barraud / Getty Images. **163** H.H. the Dalai Lama with Canon Barry Dodds (left) and Father Gerry Reynolds, Belfast, October 19, 2000. Dara Mac Donaill / The Irish Times. **164** Bill Bachman / Getty Images. **167** Rodney King and Los Angeles police officers, March 3, 1991. CNN / Getty Images. **168** Alison Wright. **171** Junko Kimura / Getty Images. **172** Ryan McVay / Getty Images. **175** Peter Cade / Getty Images. **177** Paul Thomas / Getty Images. **178** Paul O'Connor. **181** Justin Guariglia / Getty Images. **182** Popperfoto / Getty Images. **185** Ahmad Al-Rubaye / AFP / Getty Images. **186** Paul O'Connor. **189** Penny Tweedie / Getty Images. **190** Paul O'Connor. **193** Dan McCoy / Rainbow / Getty Images. **195** Andre Lichtenberg / Getty Images. **197** Paul O'Connor. **198** Verko Ignjatovic / Getty Images. **201** Martin Barraud / Getty Images. **203** Alison Wright / Corbis. **204** David Harriman / Getty Images. **207-209** Paul O'Connor. **211** Windsor & Wiehahn / Getty Images. **213** Gandee Vasan / Getty Images. **215** Donald Miralle / Getty Images. **217** Hajime Ishizeki / Getty Images. **219** Jason Hetherington / Getty Images. **221** NASA Goddard Space Flight Center Image by Reto Stöckli (land surface, shallow water, clouds). Enhancements by Robert Simmon (ocean color, compositing, 3D globes, animation). Data and technical support: MODIS Land Group, MODIS Science Data Support Team, MODIS Atmosphere Group, MODIS Ocean Group. Additional data: USGS EROS Data Center (topography), USGS Terrestrial Remote Sensing Flagstaff Field Center (Antarctica), Defense Meteorological Satellite Program (city lights). **223** Matthieu Ricard / Getty Images. **224-225** Courtesy of H.H. the 17th Karmapa. **226-228a** Ward Holmes. **228b** Courtesy of H.H. the 17th Karmapa. **229** Clemens Kuby. **230-234** Courtesy of H.H. the 17th Karmapa. **235** Paul O'Connor. **236** James Gritz / © Karmapa Foundation. **237** James Gritz / © Karmapa Foundation. **238** Paul O'Connor. **239** Robert Hansen-Sturm / © Karma Triyana Dharmachakra **240-242** Paul O'Connor. **245** James Gritz / © Karmapa Foundation.

Every effort has been made to trace copyright holders. However, if we have omitted anyone, we apologize and will, if informed, make corrections in any future editions.

RESOURCES

When not traveling, His Holiness the Seventeenth Gyalwang Karmapa, Ogyen Trinley Dorje, holds regular public audiences at his temporary residence, Gyuto Tantric Monastery in Dharamsala, India. Dharamsala, seat of the Tibetan government in exile, is situated in the foothills of the Himalayas, approximately 320 miles from New Delhi.

The best source of information on His Holiness is his official Website. Maintained by the Kagyu Office, it provides information on his current activities, schedule, projects, and personal history.

www.kagyuoffice.org

There are many Dharma Centers of the Karma Kagyu lineage worldwide and more than 100 in North America alone. For a detailed list of centers, visit:

www.kagyuoffice.org/dharmacenters.html

For more information about the historic 2008 visit of His Holiness to the United States, see:

www.karmapavisit.org